Withdrawn

INSECT WORLD

LUNA MOTHS

SANDRA MARKLE

MASTERS OF CHANGE

◤ LERNER PUBLICATIONS COMPANY MINNEAPOLIS

FOR CURIOUS KIDS EVERYWHERE

ACKNOWLEDGMENTS
The author would like to thank Dr. David Wagner, University of Connecticut, for sharing his expertise and enthusiasm. The author would also like to thank Dr. Simon Pollard, Curator of Invertebrate Zoology at Canterbury Museum, Christchurch, New Zealand, for his help with the scientific name pronunciation guides. Finally, a special thanks to Skip Jeffery, who shared the effort and joy of creating this book.

Lerner Publications Company
A division of Lerner Publishing Group, Inc.
241 First Avenue North
Minneapolis, MN 55401

Website address: www.lernerbooks.com

Library of Congress Cataloging-in-Publication Data

Markle, Sandra.
     Luna moths : masters of change / by Sandra Markle.
        p.   cm. — (Insect world)
     Includes bibliographical references and index.
     ISBN 978-0-8225-7302-9 (lib. bdg. : alk. paper)
       1. Luna moth—Juvenile literature. I. Title.
    QL561.S2M37 2008
    595.78—dc22   2007025260

Manufactured in the United States of America
1 2 3 4 5 6 – DP – 13 12 11 10 09 08

CONTENTS

WELCOME TO THE WORLD OF INSECTS—

those animals nicknamed bugs. It truly is the insects' world. Scientists have discovered more than a million different kinds—more than any other kind of animal. And they are everywhere—even on the frozen continent of Antarctica.

So how can you tell if an animal is an insect rather than a relative like the brine shrimp *(shown below)*? Both belong to a group of animals called arthropods (AR-throh-podz). The animals in this group share some traits. They have bodies divided into segments, jointed legs, and a stiff exoskeleton. This is a skeleton on the outside like a suit of armor. But one sure way to tell if an animal is an insect is to count its legs. All adult insects have six legs. They're the only animals in the world with six legs.

This book is about a kind of insect called a luna moth. A luna moth goes through amazing changes to become an adult. You are about to discover what they are.

MOTH FACT

Like all insects, a luna moth's body temperature rises and falls with the temperature around it. So it must warm up before it can fly.

OUTSIDE AND INSIDE

ON THE OUTSIDE

Some people confuse moths and butterflies. It's usually easy to tell the difference, though. Compare this Australian birdwing butterfly with the luna moth. Most moth bodies are fat and fuzzy. Most butterfly bodies are slim and smooth. Both moths and butterflies have antennae. These are the jointed, movable feelers on their heads. A butterfly's are thin with a knoblike end. Moth antennae are either threadlike or feathery. At rest, moths usually spread out their wings. Butterflies usually hold their wings together above their backs.

MOTH FACT

Like most moths, luna moths are active at night. Most butterflies are active during the day.

LUNA MOTH

BUTTERFLY

Take a look at this female luna moth. If you could touch it, its body would feel fuzzy. That's because it's covered with hairlike scales. Underneath the scales, its body would feel like tough plastic. Instead of having a hard, bony skeleton inside the way you do, an insect has an exoskeleton. This hard coat covers its whole body—even its eyes. The exoskeleton is made up of separate plates connected by stretchy tissue. This lets it bend and move. Check out the key parts of the luna moth.

ANTENNA:
One of a pair of movable feelers. Hairs on the antennae detect chemicals for taste and smell.

HEAD

THORAX

COMPOUND EYES:
What look like big s are really hundreds f eye units packed ether. These let the noth look in every direction at once.

LEGS AND FEET:
These are used for walking and holding on. All legs are attached to the thorax. Feet are claw-tipped to hold on

SCALES: Tiny scales cover and protect the wings and all body parts. They overlap like roof shingles. The scales make the wing colors.

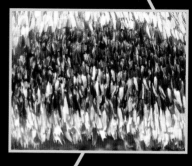

MOTH FACT

Luna moths lack simple eyes. These are small eyes to sense light from dark. Many insects have simple eyes between their compound eyes.

WINGS: Luna moths have two pairs of wings. The front and back wings flap together for flight.

SPIRACLES: These are holes down the sides of the thorax and abdomen. They let air into and out of the body for breathing.

ABDOMEN

ON THE INSIDE

Now look at the inside of an adult female luna moth.

HEART:
This muscular tube pumps blood toward the head. Then the blood flows throughout the body.

BRAIN:
This receives messages from the antennae, eyes, and sensory hairs. It sends signals to control all body parts.

NERVE CORD:
This is the insect's nervous system. It sends messages between the brain and other body parts.

OVARY:
This body part produces eggs.

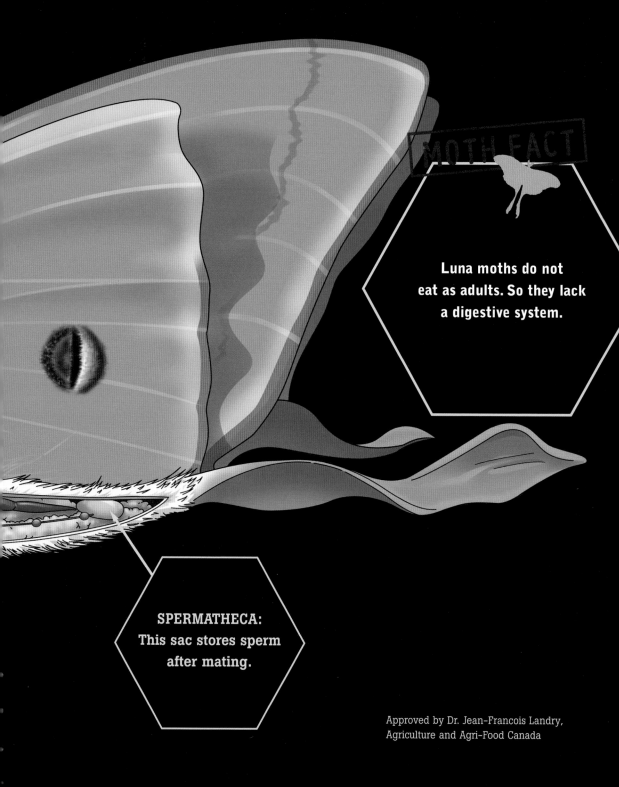

MOTH FACT

Luna moths do not eat as adults. So they lack a digestive system.

SPERMATHECA: This sac stores sperm after mating.

Approved by Dr. Jean-Francois Landry, Agriculture and Agri-Food Canada

BECOMING AN ADULT

Insect babies become adults in two ways: complete metamorphosis (me–teh–MOR–feh–sus) and incomplete metamorphosis. Metamorphosis means change. Luna moths go through complete metamorphosis. Their life includes four stages: egg, larva, pupa, and adult. Each looks and behaves very differently.

IN INCOMPLETE METAMORPHOSIS, insects go through three stages: egg, nymph, and adult. Nymphs are much like small adults. But nymphs can't reproduce.

EGG   LARVA

A luna moth is completely different during each stage of its life cycle. The way it looks is different. The way it travels from place to place is different. In some stages, it doesn't move at all. The way it gets energy from food is different too. Even the way it defends itself against predators is different. The changes that take place during complete metamorphosis are totally amazing. The process almost seems like magic.

PUPA

ADULT

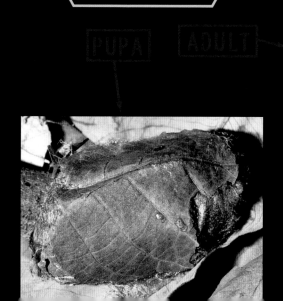

THE CYCLE BEGINS

It's a warm June night in Georgia. A female luna moth is sitting on a tree branch. She has just given off special scent chemicals called pheromones (FER-eh-mohnz). This scent is her way of attracting a mate. Male luna moths have special scent sensors on their feathery antennae. The sensors allow a male luna moth to track the female's scent.

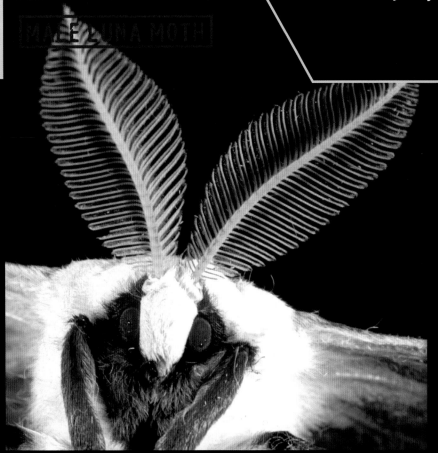

MALE LUNA MOTH

When the male finds the female luna moth, the pair mate. The male transfers a packet of sperm, male reproductive cells, into the female's body. Afterward, the male flies away. He will search for another female with which to mate. The female flies off too. But she is getting ready to lay her eggs.

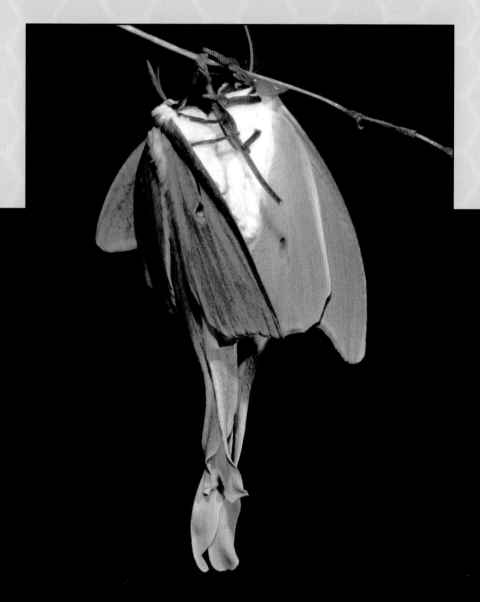

The female luna moth naturally knows to search for certain kinds of trees, like walnuts, hickories, sweet gums, and paper birches. Her young will be picky eaters. They will eat only the leaves of trees like these.

As she lays her eggs—one at a time—each egg merges with one of the male's sperm. At this time, the egg is coated with a shell-like case. The female also produces a kind of glue. She uses this glue to stick the eggs to the underside of the leaf. Under the leaf, the eggs are protected from the sun's drying rays. They are also hidden from hungry predators, like spiders.

The egg is the first stage of a luna moth's life. Nothing much seems to be happening. But inside the egg, there is a lot going on. Groups of cells are developing into a larva called a caterpillar. The developing larva gets food energy from its egg's yolk. About two weeks later, the caterpillar breaks open its egg and hatches. The second, very active stage of its life is beginning.

MOTH FACT

A female luna moth lays from four to seven eggs on a leaf. Then she moves on. She lays other batches on different trees. Even if a predator finds some, the others stay safe.

VERY HUNGRY CATERPILLARS

Like all of its brothers and sisters, this little luna moth caterpillar is hungry. All day long, except for short rests, the caterpillar eats and eats. It bites and grinds up bits of the leaves with its sharp-edged jaws. Inside, the caterpillar's body is nearly filled with its intestine, or gut. There the leaf material is changed into nutrients. This gives the caterpillar the energy it needs to grow and be active. It can only move very slowly, though. Luckily, the luna moth caterpillar's shape and coloring camouflage it, or let it blend in with its surroundings. It can hide by simply staying still.

MOTH FACT

Like most caterpillars, a luna moth caterpillar has three pairs of claw-tipped legs to grip food. And it has five pairs of stumpy legs, called prolegs, that pull it along.

LEGS

PROLEGS

BABIES STAY SAFE

Other caterpillars have other ways to stay safe. The io moth caterpillar *(below)* curls up when threatened. That makes it harder for predators to see it. It also has tufts of sharp spines on its back. If touched, these spines give off a little venom, a toxic substance. That's enough to stop most predators from biting.

MOTH FACT

Io moth caterpillars often stay in groups. They move together from one food source to another.

Cinnabar moth caterpillars also use a toxic substance to stay safe. They eat the leaves of plants that contain this poison. It builds up in their bodies and makes the caterpillars and moths poisonous to predators. The moth's bright coloring is a warning to leave it alone.

This hag moth caterpillar has a built-in disguise. Its body is shaped like a hairy spider. The hag moth doesn't look like easy prey to a would-be predator.

The elephant hawk moth caterpillar plays a trick too. Big spots on its back look like snake eyes. And when it is in danger, it rears up like a snake ready to strike. Most predators leave it alone too.

GROWING BIGGER AND BIGGER

Day after day, the luna moth caterpillar eats and eats. Even though its body looks very different from an adult luna moth's, the caterpillar also has an exoskeleton. After about a week, it outgrows its armor coat. The caterpillar needs a new exoskeleton. It uses its silk gland to spin a silk pad on a leaf. The silk gland is a tubelike part under its mouth. Next, the caterpillar hooks its claw-tipped feet to this pad and hangs upside down. The old exoskeleton splits open. The caterpillar molts, or sheds its covering. There is already a new exoskeleton underneath. It's soft at first, though. The caterpillar swallows air to stretch its new exoskeleton before it hardens. This will give the caterpillar a little extra room to grow before it has to molt again.

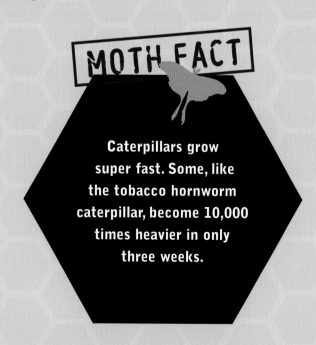

MOTH FACT

Caterpillars grow super fast. Some, like the tobacco hornworm caterpillar, become 10,000 times heavier in only three weeks.

TIME FOR A CHANGE

The luna moth caterpillar continues to eat and grow. About once a week it molts. It molts five times in all. Then one night in August, it climbs down from the tree. Once on the ground, the luna moth caterpillar spins silk again. This time, it uses the silk to stick some fallen leaves together. Inside this leaf wrapper, the caterpillar keeps on spinning. It spins until it is inside a silk bag—a cocoon. The larva is now a pupa. The third stage of its life is starting.

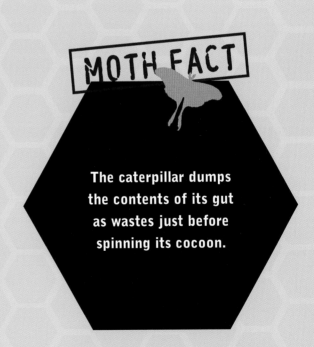

MOTH FACT

The caterpillar dumps the contents of its gut as wastes just before spinning its cocoon.

At first, the cocoon is soft. Then it becomes brown and hard. During spring and midsummer in warm Georgia, luna moth pupae become adults in just two weeks. In autumn, when it gets colder, the metamorphosis process slows down. It takes all winter for the pupa's body to change inside the cocoon. Digestive juices break down a lot of the old larval body. A new body grows from it, bit by bit. This way, the pupa turns into an adult luna moth.

MOTH FACT

In Canada, there is usually just one generation of luna moths a year. In the northeastern United States, there are usually two. And in the South, there are three.

LIFE AS AN ADULT

Winter turns to spring. On a warm March day, the adult male luna moth breaks out of his cocoon. There are hornlike bumps on his body near his front wings. These tear the cocoon's silk strands. His body also gives off a special chemical. That also helps break open a hole in the sturdy cocoon. Then the adult luna moth crawls out. He's beginning the fourth, and last, stage of his life. At first, the young male's wings are soft and folded. They had to be that way to fit inside the cocoon.

He climbs a nearby tree to reach a branch and hangs upside down. His abdomen squeezes over and over, pumping fluid into his wings. The big wings slowly unfold. Over and over, he flaps his wings while they dry and become strong. No more crawling now. He's ready to fly.

WINGS UNFOLDING

ADULTS STAY SAFE

It's evening when the male luna moth takes to the air. A screech owl spots him and flies in hot pursuit. The male has big eyes to watch for predators, so he sees the owl too. The luna moth just naturally reacts, pulling back his front wings. This flashes the big spots on his hind wings. Startled, the owl swerves and misses the moth. His defensive action worked!

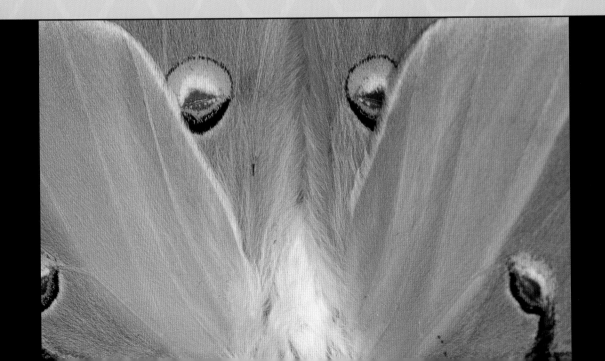

OTHER MOTH DEFENSES

Other kinds of adult moths defend themselves in other ways. Peppered moths stay safe by landing on a tree's trunk. The color of their wings blends in with the bark. So the moth seems to disappear.

The body of an adult polka-dot wasp moth is wasp-shaped. Animals hunting for prey usually avoid stinging wasps. They leave this moth alone too.

MOTH FACT

A moth's scales may save it. These scales are only loosely attached. If a moth flies into a spider's sticky web, the moth flaps its wings. The scales remain stuck. But the moth may be able to break free.

An adult tiger moth has a special defense to use against bats, its worst enemy. To find moths while flying at night, bats make high-pitched sounds. They listen for echoes, sounds bouncing off objects and prey. A tiger moth has an earlike part to listen for the bat's sounds. When the moth hears these sounds, it wiggles its thorax. This makes a clicking noise that confuses the bat. The bat can't follow its echoes to catch the moth.

CONTINUING THE CYCLE

Unlike many kinds of adult moths, an adult luna moth does not eat. It lives off stored nutrients left over from all the food it ate as a caterpillar. That means it will only live for a short time. But that is long enough to reproduce. The male flies until his antennae pick up the scent trail of a female luna moth. He follows the scent to the female.

MOTH FACT

Adult luna moths only live two to three weeks.

FEMALE

MALE

The male mates with the female he found. He dies about a week later. The female luna moth follows her natural drive to search for certain trees. Finding one she senses will be the right food for her young, she lays her eggs. She sticks them, one by one, to the bottom of leaves. She lays nearly 200 eggs in all. After laying her eggs, the female luna moth dies too.

The eggs she left behind seem to be lifeless and still. But inside, tiny caterpillars are already developing. In just a couple of weeks, new caterpillars will hatch. The process of metamorphosis is beginning again.

LUNA MOTHS AND OTHER INSECT LIFE CYCLES

LUNA MOTHS BELONG TO A GROUP, or order, of insects called Lepidoptera (lep-eh-DOP-ter-ra). That name comes from the Greek words for scales and wings. There are more than 160,000 different kinds of moths and butterflies in this group.

SCIENTISTS GROUP living and extinct animals with others that are similar. So luna moths are classified this way:

kingdom: Animalia
phylum: Arthropoda (ar-throh-POH-da)
class: Insecta
order: Lepidoptera

HELPFUL OR HARMFUL? Luna moths are both. The moth caterpillars eat leaves, so they damage plants. But caterpillars and adults are helpful because they become food for other animals, such as birds and bats.

HOW BIG is a luna moth? A luna moth's wingspan can be up to 4.5 inches (11.5 cm).

MORE INSECT LIFE CYCLES

Other insects have amazing life cycles too. Compare these insects' lives to the luna moth's.

Cicadas develop through incomplete metamorphosis. They spend a very long period as nymphs. The female deposits her eggs into slits on the bark of a twig. Shortly after hatching, the nymphs drop to the ground. They dig in and start feeding on juices from plant roots. Most kinds of cicadas spend from two to five years underground as nymphs. Some are nymphs for as long as 17 years. Finally, they tunnel to the surface. There they molt to become adults.

Aphids develop through incomplete metamorphosis. But females don't need to mate to produce babies. In the spring, only females hatch out of the eggs. They give birth to tiny nymphs. These, in turn, become adult females that produce more nymphs in the same way. Finally, in the fall, some of the nymphs become males. Then pairs mate and the females lay eggs that will survive the winter.

Caddis Flies develop through complete metamorphosis. The adult looks and acts like a moth. The wormlike larva lives on the stream bottom. It wraps itself in a silk web and sticks sand and plant bits on it. This way, the larva hides and waits to ambush prey. The larva goes through the pupa stage inside its case. Then it cuts through its case with its mandibles, pokes out legs, and swims to the surface. There, the adult breaks out and flies away.

GLOSSARY

abdomen: the tail end of an insect. It contains the parts for reproduction.

adult: the final stage of an insect's life cycle.

antennae: movable, jointed parts on the insect's head. They are used for sensing.

brain: receives messages from the antennae, eyes, and sensory hairs. It sends signals to control all body parts.

camouflage: to blend in with surroundings

caterpillar: larva form of a moth or butterfly

cocoon: the silk bag spun by a larva to completely cover itself. Once in a cocoon, a larva has become a pupa.

complete metamorphosis: a process of development in which the young look and behave very differently from the adult. Stages include egg, larva, pupa, and adult.

compound eyes: big eyes are really hundreds of eye units packed together. These let it look in every direction at once.

egg: a female reproductive cell; also the name given to the first stage of an insect's life cycle

exoskeleton: protective, skeleton-like covering on the outside of the body

head: the insect's body part that has the mouth, the brain, and the sensory organs, such as the eyes and the antennae, if there are any

heart: muscular tube that pumps blood

incomplete metamorphosis: a process of development in which the young look and behave much like small adults except that they are unable to reproduce. Stages include egg, nymph, and adult.

larva: the stage between egg and pupa in complete metamorphosis

molt: the process of an insect shedding its exoskeleton

nerve cord: the nervous system. It sends messages between the brain and other body parts.

nymph: stage between egg and adult in incomplete metamorphosis

ovary: the body part that produces eggs

pheromones (FER-eh-mohnz)**:** chemical scents given off as a form of communication

predator: an animal that is a hunter

prey: an animal that a predator catches to eat

proleg: unjointed leg extending from the caterpillar's abdomen that helps it hold on and move along

pupa: stage between larva and adult in complete metamorphosis. At this stage, the larva's body structure and systems are completely changed into its adult form.

sperm: male reproductive cell

spermatheca (spur-muh-THEE-kuh)**:** sac in female insects that stores sperm after mating

spiracles (SPIR-i-kehlz)**:** holes down the sides of the thorax and abdomen. They let air into and out of the body for breathing.

thorax: the body part between the head and the abdomen.

venom: poison produced by some insects to kill prey or attack enemies

DIGGING DEEPER

To keep on investigating luna moths, explore these books, videos, and online sites.

BOOKS

Drits, Dina. *Silkworm Moths.* Minneapolis: Lerner Publications
   Company, 2002. Investigate the life cycle of a moth that affected
   history.

List, Ilka Katherine. *Moths and Butterflies of North America.* New York:
   Franklin Watts, 2002. Check out moths and butterflies at home in
   North America.

Whalley, Paul. *Butterfly & Moth.* New York: DK Children, 2000.
   Explore over 200 different kinds of butterflies and moths—some
   exotic and rare.

VIDEO

Bug City: Butterflies and Moths. VHS. Wynnewood, PA: Schlessinger
   Media, 1998. See dramatic photography, including microscopic
   views of butterflies and moths. Hosts are Christina Ricci (*Casper*,
   The Addams Family movies) and Dr. Art Evans, director of the
   Insect Zoo at the Los Angeles County Natural History Museum.

WEBSITES

Enchanted Learning: Luna Moth

http://www.enchantedlearning.com/subjects/butterfly/activities/
printouts/Lunamothprintout.shtml

Print out a picture of an adult luna moth. Then follow the directions to color its body parts.

Fascinating Facts about Butterflies and Moths

http://www.milkweedcafe.com/fascfacts.html

Discover amazing facts about butterflies and moths. Also link to sites with microscopic views of body parts and video clips of key moments in these insects' lives.

Featured Creatures: Luna Moth

http://creatures.ifas.ufl.edu/misc/moths/luna_moth.htm

See step-by-step photos of the luna moth's development.

LUNA MOTH ACTIVITIES

PLANT A MOTH GARDEN

Want to watch adult moths feeding on night-blooming flowers? Check with a local garden center to see what night-flowering plants will grow well in your area. Here are some to consider: marjoram, chives, rockrose, thyme, thrift, evening primrose, sedum, petunias, and yuccas. Many of these plants produce a strong scent. That's perfect for attracting moths. When moths arrive, watch them in action. Does the moth feed in flight? Or does it land first? How long does a moth spend at a single flower? How many flowers does the moth visit before flying away? Remember, you won't be able to watch adult luna moths feeding. They don't eat as adults.

HUMMINGBIRD HAWK MOTH

BRING 'EM HOME ALIVE

Want to watch the magic of an adult moth come out of its cocoon? Then you'll need to go on a cocoon hunt. To find a luna moth, you'll need to be able to search from the eastern United States to the Great Plains. But there are lots of other kinds of moths that live in other places. Check online and in books. Also check what their cocoons look like. Remember for luna moth cocoons, search in the leaf litter around trees.

Once you find a cocoon, also collect some of the material around it. During this stage, the insect doesn't need food or water, but it will need to stay in its normal environment to remain healthy. Put the cocoon and other material in a large container, such as an aquarium. Insert a stick that's standing upright. It should be big enough for the adult insect to climb on. The adult will need to climb in order to spread its wings while they dry. Cover the container with a piece of window screen. Keep it outdoors where it's cool but out of wind and rain. Mist lightly with water once a week. Be sure to keep checking so you don't miss the action. Once the adult appears and its wings unfold, release it. It will need to find a mate.

Note: For a small fee, you can receive three luna or polyphemus moth cocoons by mail. These are sold by Carolina Biological Supply Company. Check online (https://www2.carolina.com) for catalog number 14–3942. Or write to the company at:

Carolina Biological Supply Company
2700 York Road
Burlington, NC 27215-3398

INDEX

PHOTO ACKNOWLEDGMENTS

The images in this book are used with the permission of: © Dwight R. Kuhn, pp. 4, 5, 12 (both), 14, 17, 25, 27, 28–29, 30, 31, 38–39, 41 (middle); © David A. Northcutt/CORBIS, pp. 7 (top), 32; © Steven David Miller/naturepl.com, p. 7 (bottom); © Ed Reschke/Peter Arnold, Inc., pp. 8–9; © Ted Kinsman/Photo Researchers, Inc., p. 9 (top); © Bill Hauser/Independent Picture Service, pp. 10–11; © Millard H. Sharp/Photo Researchers, Inc., pp. 13 (left), 36–37; © Kim Taylor/Minden Pictures, p. 13 (right); © Frederic B. Siskind, p. 15; © Stephen Cresswell, p. 19; © Stephen Dalton/Minden Pictures, pp. 21, 41 (bottom); © Troy Bartlett, p. 22; © Philippe Clement/naturepl.com, p. 23; © Rachel Hingley/naturepl.com, p. 33; © Patrick M. Lynch/Bruce Coleman, Inc., p. 34; © De Cuveland/ARCO/naturepl.com, p. 35; © Ron Austing; Frank Lane Picture Agency/CORBIS, p. 41 (top); © Hans Christoph Kappel/naturepl.com, p. 46.

Front Cover: © Altrendo/Getty Images